GLORY STORIES®
A Holy Heroes Production

MW01205873

Saint Juan Diego

"Am I not here, your mother? "

Hace 500 años en México vivía un humilde indio llamado "Cuauhtlatoatzin", que significa "águila que habla."
Nadie imaginaba que algún día se convertiría en santo!

500 years ago in Mexico, there lived a humble Indian man named "Cuauhtlatoatzin," which means "eagle that speaks."
No one imagined he would one day become a saint!

En esa época los aztecas gobernaban México. Era un pueblo muy religioso pero sirvieron a los crueles dioses falsos. Los indios vivían en constante temor de estos dioses malvados. Nadie en México sabía de Jesucristo.

At that time the Aztecs ruled Mexico. They were a very religious people, but served cruel, false gods. The Indians lived in constant fear of these evil gods. No one in Mexico knew about Jesus Christ.

En 1519, soldados españoles vinieron a México. Derrotaron a los aztecas. Los españoles trajeron sacerdotes católicos para enseñar a todos en México sobre el Dios verdadero y que Jesucristo vino a salvar a todos.

In 1519, Spanish soldiers came to Mexico. They defeated the Aztecs.
The Spanish brought Catholic priests to teach everybody in Mexico about the True God and that Jesus Christ came to save everyo

Entre las primeras personas en aprender la fe católica, eran un indio humilde y su esposa. Pidieron ser bautizados y eligieron nuevos nombres cristianos: Juan Diego y María Lucía. Juan Diego y María Lucía amaron su nueva fe. Muy temprano en la mañana, caminaban 15 millas por el desierto para asistir a la misa y clases de catecismo. A menudo era ventoso y frío, entonces Juan usualmente usaba una "tilma," un poncho indio.

among the first people to learn the Catholic faith were a humble Indian and his wife. They asked to be baptized and chose new Christian ...es: Juan Diego and Maria Lucia. Juan Diego and Maria Lucia loved their new Faith. Very early in the morning, they would walk 15 miles ...rough the desert to attend Mass and catechism classes. It was often windy and cold, so Juan usually wore a "tilma," an Indian poncho.

Un día, María se enfermó gravemente y murió. Juan Diego estaba solo, pero oraba diariamente por su esposa y se mudó con su viejo tío Bernardino para cuidarlo.

One day, Maria became very sick and died. Juan Diego was lonely,
but he prayed daily for his wife and moved in with his old uncle, Bernardino, to care for him.

Visit us online at www.HolyHeroes.co

El 9 de diciembre de 1531 Juan Diego inició su viaje largo, temprano en la mañana a la iglesia.
De repente escuchó hermosas canciones desde lo alto del cerro Tepeyac.

On December 9, 1531, Juan Diego began his long, early morning trip to church.
Suddenly, he heard beautiful songs from the top of Tepeyac Hill.

Cuando levantó la vista, escuchó la voz de una mujer llamándolo por su nombre:
"Juanito! Juan Dieguito!" Subió el cerro. En la cima vio a una hermosa señora de piel morena.

When he looked up, he heard a woman's voice call his name: "Juanito! Juan Dieguito!" ("Little John! Little John Diego!")
He climbed the hill. At the top, he saw a beautiful dark-skinned lady.

Visit us online at **www.HolyHeroes.co**

"Juanito, el más humilde de mis hijos," dijo la hermosa señora en la lengua india nativa de Juan Diego. "Soy la siempre Virgen María, Madre del Dios verdadero. Deseo que se construya una Capilla en este lugar. Ve y dile al obispo lo que deseo."

"Juanito, the most humble of my sons," the beautiful lady said in Juan Diego's native Indian language. I am the ever virgin Mary, Mother of the True God. I wish a chapel to be built in this place. Go and tell the bishop what I desire."

Juan Diego corrió para ver al obispo, Juan de Zumárraga. Pero el obispo solo dijo, "Pensaré en tu pedido."

Juan Diego ran to see the Bishop, Juan de Zumárraga. But the bishop only said, "I will give thought to your request."

Visit us online at **www.HolyHeroes.co**

Juan Diego regresó a la cima del Tepeyac donde María estaba esperando. "He fallado. Por favor, envíe a alguien más al obispo," él le suplicó. "Mi pequeño hijo," María respondió. "Hay muchos que yo podría enviar, pero usted es el que he elegido."

Juan Diego went back to the top of Tepeyac, where Mary was waiting. "I have failed. Please send someone else to the bishop," he pleaded. "My little son," Mary responded. "There are many I could send, but you are the one I have chosen."

El domingo, inmediatamente después de la Misa, Juan Diego regresó al obispo. "Debo tener una prueba de una señal de la señora antes de que pueda creerte," dijo el obispo. Exaltado Juan Diego se apresuró a regresar al cerro Tepeyac para hablar con nuestra Bendita Madre. Ella le indicó que regresara al día siguiente para recibir una señal para el obispo.

On Sunday, immediately after Mass, Juan Diego returned to the bishop. "I must have proof, a sign from the Lady, before I can beli you," said the bishop. Elated, Juan Diego rushed back to Tepeyac hill to speak to Our Blessed Mother. She instructed him to return the next day to receive a sign for the bishop.

Visit us online at **www.HolyHeroes.co**

Pero Juan Diego no regresó al día siguiente! El tío Bernardino se había enfermado y Juan Diego pasó todo el día cuidándolo. Finalmente el tío Bernardino pensó que estaba a punto de morir. El pidió a Juan a traer un sacerdote para que le confesara y lo ungiera antes de morir.

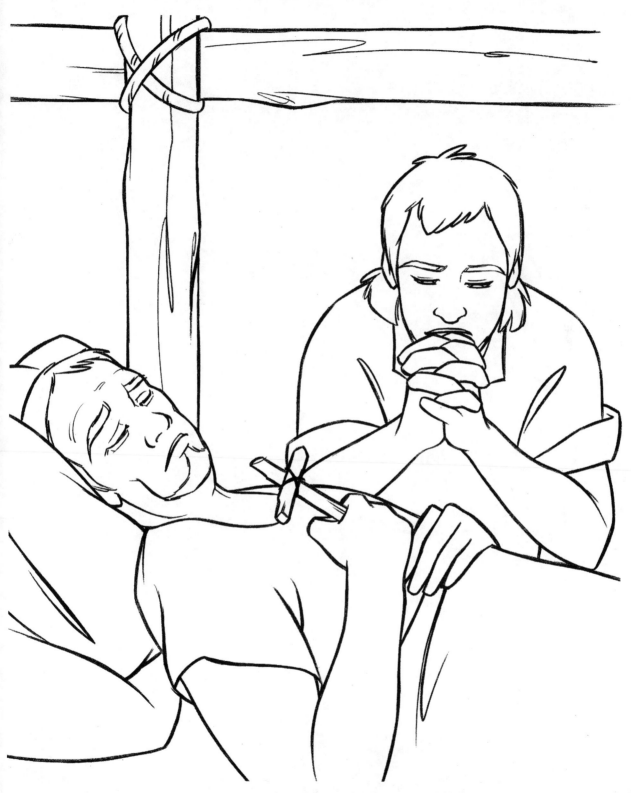

But Juan Diego did not return the next day! Uncle Bernardino had become ill, and Juan Diego spent all day nursing him.
Finally, Uncle Bernardino thought he was about to die.
He asked Juan to get a priest to hear his confession and anoint him before death.

El martes, el 12 de diciembre, Juan Diego corrió a buscar un sacerdote. Tenía que pasar el cerro del Tepeyac. Esperaba que Nuestra Señora no lo viera, así que intentó rodearlo por el otro lado.

On Tuesday, December 12, Juan Diego ran to get a priest. He had to pass Tepeyac Hill.
He hoped Our Lady would not see him, so he tried to run around it the other way.

Pero Mary bajó de la cima de la colina para encontrarse con él. "¡Mi hijito! Adonde vas?" Cayó de rodillas y comenzó a llorar. Le explicó que tenía que conseguir un sacerdote para su tío moribundo, pero le dijo que volvería mañana.

ut Mary came down from the hilltop to meet him. "My little son! Where are you going?" Juan fell to his knees and began to weep. He explained that he must get a priest for his dying uncle, but told her that he would come back tomorrow.

"No se angustie, mi hijo más pequeño. A que no estoy aquí, su madre? No estás bajo mi protección? Tu tío no morirá ahora. Su salud está restaurada en este momento. No hay necesidad de buscar un sacerdote," ella dijo. Mientras, Nuestra Señora se le apareció al Tío Bernardino. El fue curado! María le dijo, "Llámame Santa María de Guadalupe."

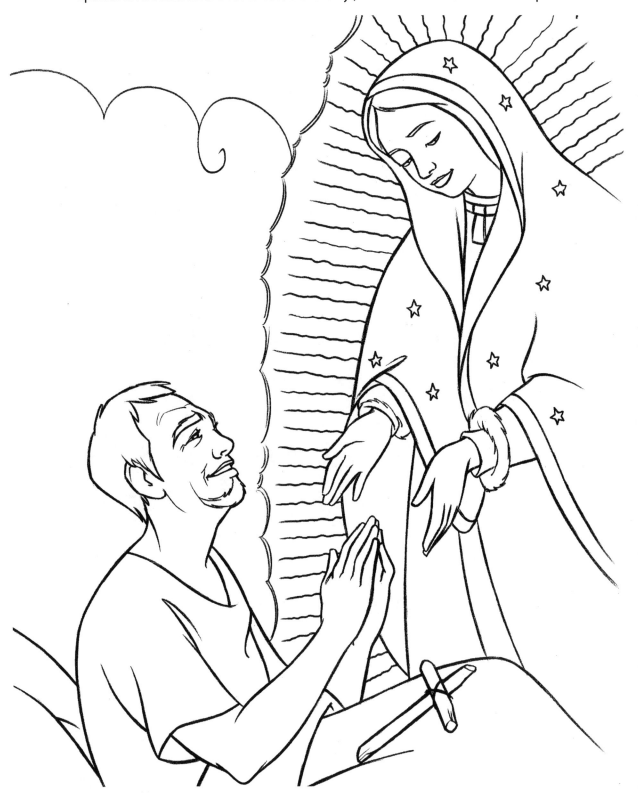

"Do not be distressed, my littlest son. Am I not here, your mother? Are you not under my protection? Your uncle will not die now. His health is restored at this moment. There is no need to get a priest," she said. Meanwhile, Our Lady appeared to Uncle Bernardin. He was cured! Mary told him, "Call me Santa Maria de Guadalupe." In English, we say, "Our Lady of Guadalupe."

Visit us online at **www.HolyHeroes.com**

"Ve ahora a la cima del cerro y corta las flores que están creciendo y luego tráemelas." Juan obedientemente subió al cerro. Para su asombro, Juan Diego encontró rosas frescas de muchos colores en la cima del cerro. Rosas en el invierno- un milagro! El reunió muchas en su tilma y las llevó al pie de la colina.

"Go now to the top of the hill and cut the flowers that are growing there, then bring them to me." Juan obediently climbed the hill. To his amazement, Juan Diego found fresh roses of many colors at the top of the hill. Roses in winter—a miracle! He gathered many into his "tilma" and carried them down the hill.

Nuestra Señora colocó cuidadosamente las flores en su tilma y luego lo cerró.
"No despliegue su tilma ni muestre estas flores a nadie más que al obispo," Ella dijo.

Our Blessed Mother carefully arranged the flowers in his tilma, then closed it around them.
"Do not unfold your tilma and show these flowers to anyone but the bishop," she said.

Visit us online at **www.HolyHeroes.com**

Juan Diego se apresuró a la casa del obispo. Juan Diego abrió la tilma para mostrarle al obispo las rosas milagrosas. Entonces apareció un milagro aún mayor: la imagen de la hermosa señora rodeada por el sol!

Juan Diego hurried to the bishop's house. Juan Diego opened his tilma to show the bishop the miraculous roses. Then an even greater miracle appeared: an image of the beautiful lady surrounded by the sun!

El Obispo Zumárraga hizo de Juan Diego un misionero de tiempo completo que trabajaba todos los días en la nueva Capilla en el cerro Tepeyac. El contó la historia de la imagen milagrosa a muchos peregrinos. Millones de mexicanos se convirtieron y fueron bautizados en la Iglesia Católica.

Bishop Zumárraga made Juan Diego a full-time missionary. Juan worked every day in the new chapel on Tepeyac Hill. He told many pilgrims the story of the miraculous image. Millions of Mexicans converted and were baptized into the Catholic Church

Visit us online at www.HolyHeroes.com

500 años después, la imagen milagrosa de Nuestra Señora sigue en la tilma! Está colgada en la nueva gran Basílica en la Ciudad de México. Al igual que Juan Diego, cualquiera que vaya allá ahora puede ver a Nuestra Señora de Guadalupe.

500 years later the miraculous image of Our Lady is still on the tilma! It hangs in the new great basilica in Mexico City. Just like Saint Juan Diego, anyone who goes there can now see "Our Lady of Guadalupe."

Helping You Bring the Joy of the Faith to Your Family

We bring you and your family inspiring stories that have motivated children (and adults) from the dawn of the Christian era: the true life stories of people just like you who lived their lives "striving to win the heavenly crown"!

Check out these and all our products online at **www.HolyHeroes.com**

Glory Stories Volume 1

While you use this coloring book, you can listen to the story of St. Juan Diego on Glory Stories Volume 1-audio CD!

Using the actual words of Our Lady of Guadalupe, this audio story extols the virtue of obedience through the miraculous story of this humble saint.

Bonus: the audio CD includes the story of Blessed Imelda Lambertini, the patroness of First Holy Communicants!

Check out more Holy Heroes coloring books!

Find samples from these coloring books on the next page!

Want even more? Get our FREE weekly faith-filled coloring pages and activities online. Sign up today at **www.HolyHeroes.com/massprep**

Visit us online at **www.HolyHeroes.com**

As Mass begins . . .

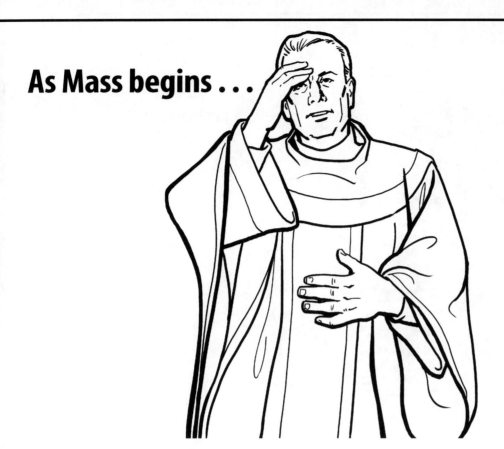

Make the Sign of the Cross with the Priest

① In the name of the
Father,

② and of the
Son,

③ and of the
Holy - Spirit

④ Amen.

Pay attention during the entire Mass:

Listen, Pray, Sing, Stand, Bow, Kneel, and Sit quietly and reverently in God's house.

Carlo began to ask his parents to bring him to Italian monasteries and convents on the weekends.
He especially loved to visit Assisi. He said, "Can you believe that St. Francis actually walked these streets?
And St. Clare, too? It's like being in Heaven."

Made in the USA
Las Vegas, NV
06 December 2023

82212701R00015